J.A.W. Wadmore

Collections for a Parochial History of Barrow Gurney

J.A.W. Wadmore

Collections for a Parochial History of Barrow Gurney

ISBN/EAN: 9783337218393

Printed in Europe, USA, Canada, Australia, Japan

Cover: Foto ©ninafisch / pixelio.de

More available books at **www.hansebooks.com**

Somersetshire

Archæological and Natural History Society.

Northern Branch.

COLLECTIONS

FOR A

PAROCHIAL HISTORY

OF

BARROW GURNEY,

BY THE

REV. J. A. W. WADMORE, (Vicar).

BRISTOL:
LAVARS AND Co,
PRINTERS, 51, BROAD STREET,
1897.

In presenting these imperfect fragments of Parochial History, the gleanings of some ten years, the writer desires to convey his thanks to the many friends, who have assisted him in his labour of love; to his father for preparing the sketches, to Bishop Hobhouse, Chancellor Rogers, Lieut. Col. Bramble, Mr. Alexander, Mr. E. Bigg, Mr. F. Were, and last but not least to the Rev. G. S. Master, not only for the use of his own notes, but also for the time and trouble he has expended on the work of revision.

Barrow Gurney,
June, 1897.

ABOUT five miles, as the crow flies, from Bristol, on the Northern slope of Broadfield Down, lying between two main thoroughfares, the Bridgwater, or Great Western road, as it was formerly called, and the road to Weston and Clevedon, stands the little village of Barrow Gurney. Beautiful as the surrounding neighbourhood is, few places can boast such variety of scenery, with its breezy upland[1] covered with gorse bracken and heather, commanding distant views of the Channel and Welsh Hills on one side, and Clifton and Bristol, with the Sodbury tumps on the other; its picturesque village lying amidst orchards in a deep valley through which flows a small stream; and its abundant woodland, from which the distant reservoirs appear like inland lakes.

The boundaries of the Parish, which consists of 2025 acres, extend from the Western reservoir past Hartcliffe rocks to Potters hill on the South; thence along the South and West sides of Barrow hill, through the Conygar[2] and Court grounds; to the lane leading to Bourton; thence through what is known as the "Wild country" on the North-east under the shadow of Dundry, to the Bridgwater Road and Reservoirs. The small stream rising at the foot of Dundry hill and known as the Elwell brook, flows through the village, supplying motive power for two mills.

[1] A rough monolith cut from Dial Quarry was erected here to commemorate the Queen's Jubilee, 1887.

[2] Cony-garth or rabbit warren. John Apadam procured a grant for free warren in his demesne lands here, as soon as they came into his possession, on the death of Oliva, mother of his wife Elizabeth. "A compleat History of Somerset, MDCCXLII."

The inhabited houses, 66 in number, lie unevenly scattered over the area, the Church occupying with the Court, an isolated position at its Western extremity.

The soil is a shallow loam upon a subsoil of clay and mountain limestone, with a patch of lias in the South-east corner of the Parish.

Amongst the Flora are several uncommon plants, Chelidonium majus, Fritillaria Meleagris, Helleborus viridis, Listera ovata, Ophrys apifera, Polemonium cæruleum. Menyanthes trifoliata, and Nymphæa alba[3] are to be found in Oatfield pond on Broadfield Down.

Narrow veins of lead, cauk, hæmatite iron, and coal have also been discovered, but not in sufficient quantities to be worked at a profit.

The list of the inhabitants, and their assessments, given in the Exchequer Lay Subsidies of I. Edward III., A.D. 1327-8 (which was a tax on 1/20 of all movable property, upon those whose goods were worth 10/- and more) is as follows :—

BAREWE.

Thomas Apadam	vi[s]
Robertus Bavent	iiij[s] qr.
Robertus Rullebury	ij[s]
Brounyng Bycheheye	viij[d]
Robertus Bercer	vij[d]
Richardus Parcarius	vij[d]
Willelmus atte Yete	ix[d] qr.
Johannes atte Broke, bercer	x[d]
[4] summa xx[e] villate predicte	xxiiij ,, vij[d]

[3] Som. Arch. vol. xxxix, p.96, Rev. F. Murray's. Flora of Somerset.
[4] Som. Rec. Society, vol. iii, pp. 94, 95.

The present gross estimated rental is £17,307 ; the rateable value £14,705 ; while from the Apportionment of rent-charge in lieu of Tithes, it appears "that the land subject to Tithe is 2000 acres, and the Rent-charge £245.

The population in 1808 was 203, in 1831 279, 1841 303, 1851 406,[5] 1861 321, 1871 361, 1881 302, and at the last census in 1891 338,[6] so that, contrary to general experience, the population shows a gradual growth in spite of rural leakage.

Among field names, which are as varied as the character of the village, occur Hevens hill, Dead hill, Church close, Bobbin slade, Lipstone, Pax pit, Winyard, and a miscellaneous assortment of Clouds, Waterslides, Fillies, &c. The old " Pound " now converted into a garden, stands in the rear of a carpenter's shop on the Bridgwater road.

[5] During the construction of the old Reservoir.

[6] Barrow Court being unoccupied.

BARROW COURT, SOMERSET.

BARROW GURNEY.

THE Manor at the time of the Domesday Survey formed a part of the vast estates of the Bishop of Coutances, upon whom the Conqueror bestowed, with other manors, almost the whole of the hundred of Portbury.[7] The entry runs thus : —

"Nigel holds of the Bishop, Berve. Edric held it in the time of King Edward, and gelded for ten hides. The arable is fourteen carucates. In demesne are two carucates, and three servants, and fifteen villanes, and seven cottagers. There is a mill of five shillings rent, and thirty-five acres of meadow, and thirty acres of pasture. Wood one mile long, and one furlong broad. It was and is worth ten pounds."

Reverting to the Crown upon the death or attainder of the Bishop, it was conferred by William Rufus upon Robert, second son of Harding, the well-known founder of the great family of Berkeley.[8]

Robert Fitz-Harding born in the year 1085, was a merchant, and Provost of the City of Bristol, the first Lord Berkeley, and founder of the great monastery of S. Augustine, and dying in 1170, was buried there between the stalls of the Abbot and Prior. By his wife Eva, who founded the nunnery of the 'Magdalens' and died 1170, he had five sons and two daughters, (1) Henry ; (2) Maurice Lord Berkeley ; (3) Nicholas, lord of Tykenham; (4) Robert, called 'De Were,' lord of Beverston, Kingweston, English-combe

---

[7] Bishop Hobhouse' Domesday map of Somerset. Somerset Arch. Journ. vol. xxxv.

[8] Smyths' lives of the Berkeleys. Vol. 1, p. 19. His arms are described as ' *Gules a chevron argent.*'

and Barrow; and (5) Thomas, a priest. Robert married first[9] Hawisia daughter of Robert de Gournay, by whom he had a daughter, Eva ; and secondly Alice, daughter of Robert de Gaunt, by whom he had a son, Maurice,[10] styled ' de Gaunt' from his mother. Maurice founded the hospital of S. Mark Billeswick, and the Gaunt's Chapel, where he lies buried beneath a stone effigy,[11] clad in chain mail and surcoat, crosslegged, and sheathing his sword. The Manor reverted to his half-sister Eva de Gournay, who became heiress of the great families of Fitz-Harding, Gournay, Gaunt, and Paganel, married Thomas de Harpetre, lord of Farrington and Harpetre, and may possibly have been the foundress of Barrow Mynchin.[12] She died about 1216.

Their son Robert de Harpetre, adopting the surname of Gournay [13] from his mother, appended it to his manors of Farrington and Barrow. He was a benefactor to the hospital of S. Mark, and dying in 1269, was buried there ; his crosslegged effigy in chain armour differing but slightly from that of his uncle. "He married Hawisia de Longchamp"[14] by whom he had issue, Anselm and John, the latter dying s.p.

Anselm de Gourney married Sibilla, daughter of Hugh de Vivonne,[15] and left three sons, John, Robert, and Thomas. The last was father of Sir Thomas de Gournay, one of the murderers of King Edward II, and beheaded 1333. The second is now represented by the Earl of Egmont,[17] while John[18] married Oliva, daughter of Lord Lovel[16] of Castle Cary, and died 1291, leaving a daughter and heiress,

[9] Smyths' lives of the Berkeleys. Vol. 1, p. 52.

[10] He had a life grant from the Crown of the Manor of Barewe, conceded his by sister, Eva de Gurney, A.D. 1214. Proceedings of Archæol. Inst. at York, p. 80. Rev. H. M. Scarth.

[11] Figured in Glouc. Archæol. Journ. Vol. xv, pp. 89, 90.

[12] Somerset Archæol. Journ. xii, 2, 50, 125.

[13] Arms of Gournay. " Paly of six, or and azure." Harpetre. " Argent, a cross humetty flory at the ends in saltire gules."

[14] Arms of Longchamp. " Or three crescent gules, each charged with a mullet of five points argent."

[15] Arms of Vivonne. " Gules, on a chief argent a label of three points of the first."

[16] Arms of Lovel. " Or. crousily crosslets a lion rampant ."

[17] House of Yvery, Vol. II, p. 533.

[18] Johannes de Gournay tenet villam de Barwoe per servicium unius feodi de Anselino de Gurnay et idem Anselinus de honore comitis. Glouc. et comes de rege. Kirby's Quest. Somerset Archæological Society, iii, 29.

3

Elizabeth de Gournay, who by her marriage to Sir John Ap Adam[19] lord of Beverston and Kingweston, when only sixteen years of age, carried Barrow to that family. He died in 1318 and was succeeded by his son and heir,

Sir Thomas Ap Adam, who failing issue by his marriages, first to Joan Inge, and secondly to Alice Basset, conveyed the manor in 1331, with that of Beverston, to

Thomas, third Lord Berkeley[20] and Margaret his wife, in whose family it remained till the 34th year of the reign of Henry VIII, when it was alienated by the possessor Sir John Berkeley with other landed estates, to Peter Compton, Esq. the only son[21] of Sir Wm. Compton, Kt., a friend and favourite of King Henry VIII. He married Anne, daughter of George Talbot, Earl of Shrewsbury, and was succeeded by his only son,[21] Sir Henry Compton,Kt.[22] of Wynyate, Co. Warwick, summoned to Parliament 1572 as Baron Compton of Compton. He married first Frances, daughter of Francis Earl of Huntingdon, and had issue, William second Lord Compton, created Earl of Northampton 1618, who in 1596 sold this manor to

William Clerc, gent, the purchaser of Barrow Mynchin, who married Frances 2nd daughter of Hugh Brook of Ashton Philips, Esq., and resold it three years later to

William Hanham and others, who about 1603-4 conveyed it to

Francis James, L.L.D., Chancellor of Wells, Judge of the Court of Audience of the Archbishop of Canterbury, and of the High Court of Chancery. He died in 1615, and his sons[23] Francis, and William sold it in 1626, to

[19] Johannes Appadam tenet unum feodum in Barwe de comite Gloucester. Kirby's Quest 1302-3, Som. Rec. Soc. III, 42. Arms of Apadam, "*Argent on a cross gules five mullets or.*"
[20] Arms of Berkeley. "*Gules, a chevron between ten crosses pattée argent.*" Smyth's lives of the Berkeleys. Vol. I, pp. 326, 334, 350.
[21] Burke's Peerage, Northampton.
[22] Arms of Compton. "*Sable three close helmets argent.*"
[23] By his will dated May 27th, 1612, Barrowe was bequeathed to his eldest son Francis, and Kingston Seamore to his son William, with reversion to survivor.

Robert Cotterell, whose daughter and heiress married—Hazle, son of William and Johanne Hazle of the old Court of Barrow Gurney.

Their daughter and heiress Magdalen married Benjamin Tibbot[24] of Dundry, who left two sons, John and Nathaniel, both of whom died vitâ patris, and three daughters (1) Alice, (2) Mary who died 1652, and (3) Joan.

John died 1674, leaving a daughter Ruth, who married William Gore 2nd of that name, eldest son of Sir Thomas Gore, Kt., of Barrow Court, and Philippa his wife. Ruth died 1689, leaving an only daughter Mary, who married Anthony Blagrave of Southcot, Esq., 2nd son of John Blagrave of Reading, Esq., M.P.[25]; by Hester, youngest daughter of Wm. Gore, Esq., the purchaser of Barrow Mynchin from the Dodingtons. They had two sons, (1) John Blagrave, Esq., who died without issue, and (2) Anthony Blagrave, Esq., who died 1778, leaving two daughters and co-heirs, Frances and Anne, the latter wife of Rev. James Cullum, the former of John Blagrave of Watchfield in Shrivenham, Esq., of another branch of the family. He died in 1827, leaving four sons and six daughters, one of whom married Dr. Martin Joseph Routh, President of Magdalen College, Oxon. The eldest son,

John Blagrave, Esq., of Calcot Park, Berks, married 1827, Mary Anne, daughter of Henry Parsons, Esq., and relict of the Rev. Matthew Robinson, brother of Lord Rokeby, and secondly Georgiana, daughter of Sir Wm. Rowley, 2nd Bart. of Tendring Hall, Suffolk, but dying without issue in 1867, was succeeded by

Anthony Blagrave, Esq., who married Rachel, daughter of Thomas Yates, Esq., and relict of John Dailey, Esq., and died 1860 leaving, with a daughter,

John Henry Blagrave of Calcot Park, Esq., High Sheriff of Berks, 1870, who married 1844 (1) Sarah Cooper daughter of Richard

[24] Arms of Tibbot. "*Barry of gules and argent, a fesse embattled sable.*" Coll, ii 108.
[25] Arms of Blagrave. "*Or, on a bend sable 3 legs in armour couped at the thigh, and erased at the ancle ppr.*"

5

Sayers of Greenwood, Co. Dublin, Esq., (she died 1865, and was buried at Barrow;) and (2) Agnes, daughter of the Rev. Henry Pole and relict of George Smith Thornton, Esq., who died without issue, and was buried at Tylehurst. By his first wife he had, with six daughters, three sons,(1)John Anthony, born 1846, died 1850,(2) Henry Barry, born 1848, married Margot Moran, (3) John Gratwicke, born 1853, who inherited the manor under his father's will (1892, proved 1895). John Henry Blagrave, Esq., died June, 1895, and was buried at Tylehurst, æt 84.

The History of the Benedictine nunnery of Barrow Mynchin, The Nunnery which occupied the site of the present Court house, has been so exhaustively treated by the Rev. T. Hugo, F.S A.,[26] the well-known antiquary, that a brief summary of his paper is all that is here necessary. The date of its foundation was anterior to 1212, in which year[27] Hugh, Bishop of Lincoln, amongst other religious bequests for the good of his soul, left ten marks " domui monialium de Berwe.' Mr. Hugo is probably correct in assuming that Eva de Gournay, the grand-daughter and heiress of Robert Fitz-Harding, first Lord Berkeley, was its foundress, for her son Robert, who adopted his mother's name of Gournay, held amongst other tenures, of the Earl of Gloucester, the "Manor of Barwe." She died before 1230. Of its actual size and dimensions there is absolutely no trace. The endowment was a slender one, consisting of little more than the lands immediately adjacent to the priory, to which was added a rent-charge or pension of £1. 6s. 8d. from the Church of Twerton, near Bath.[28] In fact so small was the income, that the poor nuns of Barowe were more than once exempted from taxation. The lords of the manor as patrons retained authority over the religious house, which was not allowed to elect a superior without their consent, while the Prioress and nuns of Barrow were bound to find pasture and fold for 160

[26] Somerset Archæological Society, vol. xii. 2, p. 46.
[27] See will. Collinson's Somerset vol ii., p. 310.
[28] Mentioned in Pope Nicholas' Ecclesiastical Taxation, A.D. 1291.

sheep belonging to the Lords of Berkeley. This obligation, however, was remitted in 9 Edward III. on "the nuns promising to keep the anniversary of the Lord Maurice, Thomas the 3rds. father, on the last day of May, and the anniversary of the Lady Eve his mother, on December 5th, yearly, and likewise the anniversary days of himself, and of Margaret his wife, after they are departed this life, &c."[29] In 1361, Richard de Acton, chevalier, "gave and assigned eight messuages, one shop, six tofts, ten acres of meadow, and eight of pasture, in Wells and Barwegorney, to the Prioress and nuns of Minchin Barewe, to provide a chaplain for the celebration of Divine Service every day for ever, at the altar of the Blessed Virgin Mary, in the Priory Church, for the health of the donor in life and death, and for all the faithful departed." This was further supplemented in 1369, by a grant of "72 acres of arable land, and seven acres of meadow, with appurtenances, to the Prioress and Convent, worth 40/- for providing a lamp which should be constantly burning before the High Altar in honour of the Body of our Lord," the deed of donation being witnessed at Westminster by King Edward III.; while in the same year John Blanket of Bristol assigned "2 messuages, 2 shops, and 2 gardens contiguous to the said shops in the City of Bristol" to the Sisterhood, "for perpetually providing bread and wine for all masses at the High Altar, and other works of piety, for his soul and body's health." Among the list of subsequent benefactors we find the name of Robert Cheddre, who included the " Sisters of Mochenburgh 'in his will, 1382; Walter Darby, burgess of Bristol, 1385; William Hervy of the same city, 1393, and Gilbert Hareclife, who gave to Joan Panes prioress, 2 acres in an enclosure called Chappel-meade, with reference to which in 1403 the Prioress and Convent solicited the King to grant letters of pardon for " having

[29] Smyth's Lives of the Berkeleys, vol. 1, p. 334.
[30] Wells Wills Weaver, p. 6. From this we find that several smaller bequests were made, viz., in 1533 Thomas Crosse bequeaths to the "Hye Beame" of the said Church ijd. our Lady ijd., witnessed by Sir Richard Wryght, priest of Barrow. In the same year William Crosse husbandman, makes a similar bequest.

appropriated and occupied without license a close of land called Chapels Croft," an offence which ultimately the King overlooked, confirming the gift.[30]

The discipline and finances of the house seem to have given rise to considerable difficulty. As early as 1315 Bishop John de Drokensford, in a letter dated at Chu (Chew) directs "the prioress of Bargh, on pain of excommunication and suspension, to observe and keep certain injunctions, to devote herself to the worship of God, and the government of the house; the Prioress and nuns are to eat and sleep together, go about in pairs, not absent themselves without leave, observe silence, and live in charity and love, duly attending Service at the appointed hours." This was followed by a letter authorising John de Sutton to act as visitor and adviser. In 1316 the Prioress, whose name unfortunately does not transpire, died, and Johanna de Gournay, of founder's kin, probably a daughter of Robert or Thomas de Gournay, was elected her successor. She was professed July 26th, 1317, in the chapel of the Bishop's Palace at Banwell (where a modern stained glass window commemorates the event), and received imposition of hands in company with three other sisters, Agnes Saint de Merays, Milburga de Derneford, and Basilida de Suttone.

The House fell into such poverty and decay under her administration, in spite of the admonition of the Rectors of Chu, Harpetre and Backwell, that the Bishop was compelled to require her resignation, which was confirmed by a memorandum in the register of Bishop John de Drokensford, dated the third of May. Leave was then given to the nuns to appoint a successor, and their choice fell upon the sub-Prioress Agnes de Sancta Cruce, who died after a brief tenure of 3 years. Basilia de Suttone was then unanimously elected, and succeeded to office after taking the oath of canonical obedience. On the 17th June, 1340, Prioress Basilia de Suttone was numbered with her predecessors, and the Sisters, after a meeting in the Chapter

House, gave their votes in favour of Juliana de Groundy, who was inducted into office August 20th. She either died or resigned in 1348, and was succeeded by Agnes Balun, a nun of the house, who in turn gave place to Joanna Panes. Before 1410 another change had evidently taken place, as we find Margaret Fitz Nichol, one of that branch of the great Berkeley family known as "De Tickenham," petitioning to be released from her duties on account of her advanced age and precarious health. Her request was granted, but she was admonished that neither age nor infirmity were excuses for non-compliance with the rules of her order. Nothing further worth notice occurred till 1432, when the patronage having lapsed to the Bishop, John Stafford, he appointed Johanna Stabler to be prioress, and conferred on her the rights and appurtenances of the Mynchin. She was succeeded by Agnes Leveregge.[31] In 1501 the Priory received another head of the name of Dame Isabella Cogan, who was elected in the Church which is called in this solitary instance (the only one prior to the Reformation), " The Conventual Church of the Priory of the Holy Trinity of Mynchin Barowe."[32] She entered into a lease with John Babor of Chewstoke of the Rectory, tithes, and tithe barn of Twiverton for 60 years, and received upon her retirement in 1535 an annuity of £4, payable to herself or her trustee, Sir Edward Gorges Knt., in the parish church of Wraxall. Her successor was Katherine Bowle, or Boule, the last Prioress, for on September 19th 1536 the dissolution formally took effect, and the unfortunate inmates were turned out, without, so far as can be ascertained, any compensation, a pension of £5 being allowed to the Prioress only. The names of the poor nuns so unceremoniously deprived of their home, have been unexpectedly brought to light by Dr. Gasquet, the painstaking Author of " Henry VIII. and the English Monasteries," and proved to be Elizabeth Gregory, Elizabeth Dunne, Margaret

[31] About this lady there is some doubt, her name is introduced on the authority of Collinson, but is not confirmed by any entry in the Episcopal Register.

[32] Somerset Archæological Society. Proceedings vol. xxxviii., p. 334.

Tunnell,[33] Anne Hoper, Joanna Bowey, Agnes Latymer, Katharine Bowle prioress, Elizabeth Cogan, late prioress.

In the year 1537, the site of the priory with its buildings and precincts, together with the rectory and advowson of the Church, were granted to John Drew, of the city of Bristol, on lease for 21 years, at the annual rent of £5. 1s. 8d. for the buildings and land, and £8. 14s. 1d. for the profits of the Rectory saving a Rent charge of £6. for the stipend of a Chaplain serving the cure of the Parish Church.[34]

John Drewe was a citizen and merchant of Bristol, styled "Armiger" in the documents; his coat of Arms[35] was in Collinson's time,[36] 1791, to be seen in the north chancel window; he converted the domestic buildings into a suitable residence, for Leland, who visited the spot in or before 1539, records, that "here was of late a nunnery, now made a fair dwelling-place by Drue of Brightstow," [37] and six years later sold the property to William Clerc, the premises being valued at £15. 18s. 1d. per annum for the sum of £160.

The Court.

William Clerc entered into possession in 1558 He is styled in the conveyance "generosus," his claim to coat armour being disallowed at the Visitation of 1591[38]; so Collinson must be mistaken in attributing to him the shield[39] now in the South external wall of the Court aisle, and previously over the East window of the North Porch. His first wife was Frances d. of Hugh Brook,[40] of Ashton-Philips, Esq. Administration of his effects was granted to Dorothy his relict

[33] Sir William Webster, Chaplain of Bourton, by his Will, 1535, leaves to Margaret Tunnell, Mynchin of Barrow, his coffer and a payre of bedes of Whytte Ivory, to Sir John, of Barrow, his best chyrkyn, to the Mynchyn's of Barrow vjs. viijd., Dame Elizabeth Cogan, same tyme prioress iijs. iiijd. Weavers Wells Wills, p. 10.

[34] The Priory property at Wells was purchased in the following year by John Aylworth for £35 19s., and a mill in Barrow Gurney was leased to Robert Payton for 21 years at a rent of 20s. per annum.

[35] "*Argent, two chevrons sable between three roses gules seeded or.*" Mary Wickham.

[36] Collinson's Somerset. ii., p. 312.

[37] Leland's Itinerary Som. Arch. Jour. xxiii., 132.

[38] Som. Arch. Journal xxiii., 31.

[39] "*On a bend between two lions rampant, three escallop shells*" a slight variation of the coat of Norton, of Abbots Leigh. Coll. ii. 312.

[40] Arms. "*Gules on a chevron or three lions rampant, sable.*" Coll. ii. 300.

in 1621[41]. His son Christopher sold the property to Francis James, D.C.L., by which transaction the lordship of the Manor and the ownership of the Court became merged in the same person.

Dr. Francis James was the son of John James of Little On, in Staffordshire; his brothers being respectively :—Edward James, Merchant, and Dr. William James, Bishop of Durham, 1606-1617, whose son Francis, was named after his uncle. He was Fellow of All Souls Coll Oxon ; M.P. for Dorchester, 1592 ; a Master in Chancery ; Judge of the Court of Audience of the Archbishop of Canterbury ; Chancellor of the Dioceses of Bristol, and Bath and Wells, and donor of the great West window of the Abbey Church of Bath,[42] 1612. His first wife was Elizabeth, who died in Bristol, and was interred in S. Mark's Chapel, where there is a monument to her memory.[43] He married secondly Blanche, relict of William Billingsley, daughter and heir of Francis Gunter,[44] of London, by Jane, daughter of Edward Lloyd, of Oswestry, and widow of Edward Southworth, father of Thomas and Henry Southworth, half-brothers of Blanche James. By her he had four sons and five daughters, all of whom are represented on his monument. He may possibly have been the builder of the Court house. He died March 1616, leaving directions in his will dated May 1613, and proved May, 1616, that he should be " buried in ye Chancel of Barrowe, in the upper end of that Ile which was heretofore the Church or Oratory of the Nonnes, and is now belonging to the lordship of Barrow, and a monument to be erected by his wife, Blanche." He left £50 to the poor of Bristol, " where he lived many comfortable years," and the same to Wareham, Dorchester, and Wells, £400 to each of his five daughters, Jane, Catherine, Philippa, Mary, and Margaret:

---

[41] Somerset wills, iii. 32.

[42] Miscellanea Genealogica iv. 82, 84. Somerset Wills, i. 39.

[43] " Here lieth the body of Elizabeth James, late wife of Francis James, D.C.L. a 'woman for her excellent virtues and singular wisdom to be equalled by few of her sex. As she lived very religiously and godly, so she died May 1. 1599. "Charissimæ conjugi posuit superstes maritus." Barrett's Bristol, p. 350."

[44] Arms of Gunter, "*Sable, three gauntlets argent in chief a crescent or for diff.*"

,, James, " *Sable, a dolphin naiant embowed below 3 crosses crosslet or.*"

Barrow to his eldest son Francis [45] (in ward 1623, died 1629.)
Kingston-Seymour to his son William : his younger sons were
Edward born after 1613, and John : his papers, with characteristic
prudence, were committed to the flames. His son Francis, soon
after succeeding to the estate, sold it to Sir Francis Dodington and
John his son, in 1626. [46]

Sir Francis Dodington, [47] Knight, eldest son of John Dodington
and Catherine his wife, Sheriff for Somerset in 6 Charles I, did not
long reside at Barrow Court. Obliged by the destruction of the
Royalist party, to flee the country, he sailed to France, where
he is said to have maintained himself by selling English knives
and buckles, till a French widow took compassion upon him,
and married him. His first wife was Anne, daughter, and heiress
of Sir William Hoby, [48] and relict of John Sydenham, Esq., by
her he had a son and heir John, who married Hester, daughter
of Sir Peter Temple, Bart., and died in his father's lifetime,
leaving a son, George, who succeeded Sir Francis in the estate
of Dodington, but dying without issue, the property devolved
eventually upon Earl Temple. Sir Francis Dodington and John
his son sold the Barrow Estate in 1659 to William Gore, of Morden,
Surrey, and Gilston, Herts., Esq., in whose family it remained for
upwards of 200 years.

William Gore, second son of Sir John Gore, Knight, Lord
Mayor of London, 1624, and Hester, his wife, daughter of Sir
Thomas Campbell, Alderman of London, married Jane, daughter of
Thomas Smith, Esq., of Tedworth, Hants. [49] They both died and
were buried here, he in 1662, and she in 1698. They had issue

[45] A portion of his gravestone, found in the churchyard, is now let into the floor of the Court chapel and bears the date of his death.

[46] Coll. ii. 311.

[47] Coll. iii. 518-9. Arms. "Sable, three bugle horns argent," are carved on Dodington Church, and depicted in the windows of the Manor House there. Vis. of Som. 1623. Harleian Soc. p. 33.

[48] Arms. "Argent a fesse sable between 3 hobbies, ppr, belled and jessed or. Pap. 731."

[49] Som. Wills v. 85, Monument in S. Aisle. Arms of Smith. "Azure, two bars between three pheons or."

(1) Sir Thomas Gore, (2) William Gore, of S. Paul's, Covent Garden, Esq., who died 1724, æt 85, without issue, and was buried here, (3) John Gore, of S. Paul's Covent Garden, Esq., buried here 1724, æt, 83,(4) Gerard Gore, of the County of Northampton, Esq., who married and had issue ; (5) Jane Gore, who married first John Travell Esq., and secondly Newton, Esq., (6) Hester Gore, the wife of John Blagrave, of Reading, Esq., M.P., by whom she had two sons and a daughter, Hester.

Sir Thomas Gore of Barrow Court, Knight, the eldest son, died 1675 and was buried here.[50] He married Philippa, daughter of Edward Tooker[51] Esq., sister and co-heir of Sir Giles Tooker, of Maddington Wilts, created a baronet 1664, died 1665, and by her, (who married secondly at Barrow, 1701, Mr. Joseph Earle[52] called 'Knight' in Wills of Som., Series v. p. 89, and was buried here, 1703); had issue, (1) William Gore the 2nd of that name, of Barrow Court, (2) Thomas Gore, bapt. 1666, (3) Edward Gore, Esq. (4) John Gore, bapt. and buried here, 1673, and 1675 ; and four daughters, (1) Jane, bapt., 1667, wife of Richard Baskerville, of Richardston, Wilts, Esq., (2) Mary, bapt. 1669, wife of George Speke, of Hazlebury, Wilts, Esq., (3) Anne, bapt. 1670, died 1729,[53] wife of Thomas Bourne, Esq., and (4) Philippa, bapt. 1674.

William Gore, of Barrow Court, eldest son of Sir Thomas, bapt. 1665, and buried here 1718, was twice married, first to Ruth, daughter of John Tibbot of Dundry, lord of the manor of Barrow Gurney, who died 1689, leaving an only daughter and heir, Mary, who married Anthony Blagrave, of Southcot, Esq. ; and secondly, to Mary Crisp[54] who died 1705, leaving three surviving sons, and

[50] Somerset Wills, v 88, and Register.
[51] Arms of Tooker. "*Vert, on a bend engrailed argent three body hearts gules.*" Mrs. Mary Tooker, daughter of Sir John Hungerford, of Down Ampney, Gloucester; married 1st, William Platt, Esq. 2ndly Edward Tooker, of Barrow Gurney. Buried at Highgate, 1686.
[52] Compare Annals of Bristol, where in 1681, Thomas Earle, Mayor, and John Knight, Sheriff, were knighted.
[53] See Will—Somerset Wills, v 81.
[54] Buried in vault under the Court Chapel, in a leaden coffin, with arms embossed on the lid. "*Or on a chevron sable, five horseshoes argent.*"

two daughters, the rest dying in infancy, (1) Thomas, born 1692, married Mary, daughter of William Ward, of Morpeth, Esq., and died 1728, leaving three sons and a daughter, who all died in youth ; (2) Edward, born 1696, married Elizabeth (buried here 1718) surviving her only three years ; (3) William, born 1700, married Mary May, and died without issue 1769 [55] ; of the daughters, Hester twin with Edward, born 1696, died unmarried 1721, and Anne, born 1698, married Thomas Speke of Haselbury, Wilts, Esq. Issue failing in the direct line, the property reverted to John, eldest son of Edward Gore, of Flax-Bourton, Esq., (third son of Sir Thomas), who married Arabella, sister and co-heir of Sir John Smyth,[56] of Long Ashton, Bart., and died 1742, aged 70, leaving by his wife, who died 1748, æt 48, the aforesaid John and Edward.

John Gore succeeded to the Estate in 1768. He married, 1st Temperance, 2ndly Mary Jenkins, both of whom died without issue, and were buried here respectively in 1780 and 1788, dying himself in 1796. His only brother, Edward, who succeeded him, married Barbara, widow of Sir Edward Mostyn, Bart., daughter and sole heir of Sir George Browne[57] of Kiddington Park co Oxford, by Lady Barbara Lee, daughter of the first Earl of Lichfield, and dying 1801, æt 72, left issue,

(1) William Gore, of Newton S. Loe, Esq., who assumed by Royal license the surname and arms of Langton, on his marriage 1783 with Bridget, daughter and heir of Joseph Langton,[58] of Newton Park, Esq., by whom he had seven children ; and (2) the Rev. Charles Gore born 1764, who succeeded ; he married 1795, Harriett, daughter of Richard Littell,[59] Esq., and by her, who was buried here 1840, aged 66, left at his death in 1842, æt 76.,

[55] Somerset Wills, v. 87.

Arms of May. "*Gules a fesse between eight billets or.*"
[56] Arms of Smyth. "*Gules, on a chevron between three cinque foils argent, as many leopards faces sable.*"

[57] Arms of Browne. Sable on a bend, cotised argent, three lions passant of the first.

[58] Arms of Langton. Quarterly sable, and or, a bend argent.

[59] Arms of Littell. Sable, a pillar, ducally crowned between two wings expanded and joined to the base or.

(1) Montague Gore of Barrow Court, Esq., born 1800, M.P., for Barnstaple and High Sheriff of Somerset 1852, who died unmarried, 1864 ; (2) The Rev. William Charles Gore, minister of Barrow 1829-41, who died at S. Kitts 1842, aged 41 ; (3) Richard Hugh Gore, (whose monumental tablet tells its own story,) buried 1826, æt 23 ; (4) Francis James Gore died 1823, aged 27 ; (5) John Sigismond Gore, 27th Foot, died 1823, aged 21 ; (6) The Rev. George Gore, Rector of Newton S. Loe.

In 1856, the property was sold by Montague Gore, Esq., to John Henry Blagrave, Esq., who disposed of it in 1881 to Antony Gibbs, of Tyntesfield Esq. ; from whom it passed into the hands of the present proprietor, Henry Martin Gibbs Esq., second surviving son of William Gibbs, Esq., the well-known munificent churchman. Henry Martin Gibbs, Esq.,[60] married in 1882 Emily Anna, daughter of the Ven. William Otter, Archdeacon of Lewes, and has had issue seven sons and two daughters, one of the latter deceased.

The Court house, in spite of the scant justice meted out by the Rev. T. Hugo, F.S.A., who calls it "a plain and uninteresting structure of three stories in height," may be assigned to the close of Queen Elizabeth's reign, and is a good specimen of the style of that period. It stands on or near the site, and was erected from the material of the ancient Nunnery of which a fine old stone barn with open roof and transept-like entrance is the only existing relic. Engravings of the Court in Collinson's Somerset,[61] and Rutter's North Somerset,[62] give a good idea of its appearance prior to the extensive alterations and improvements which have been carried out by the present owner, who has restored it in a true conservative spirit, retaining all that was worthy of preservation, and enabling it once more to take its place among the finest country seats of Somerset.

[60] Arms of Gibbs. "*Argent, three battle axes erect within a bordure nebule sable.*"
,, Otter. "*Or, on a bend gules, gutté déau, between two crosses pattée of the second three crescents argent.*"
[61] Vol 11, p. 308.
[62] p. 17.

The house, approached by a straight carriage drive, (the iron
gates marking in all probability the East boundary of the
Nunnery enclosure), retains its original arrangement of a passage
from the entrance porch to the interior, with a large hall opening out
on the right, while the dining room on the left has superseded the
ancient offices which were there before 1881. At the South end of the
hall, (in a window of which are a few fragments of stained glass, representing the head of the Saviour in a cruciform nimbus, and the mono-
gram A.H.) was the minstrel's gallery, looking out into the porch,
which is generally attributed to the time of James I. though the columns
have a stunted appearance, as if they had been adapted to suit their
present position. The façade bears the Gore arms, supported by figures
of Flora and Pomona. At the end of the passage is the staircase with a
fine ceiling of hand-wrought plaster, and a deeply fretted pendant,
leading to the morning room on the right, with old oak panelling, and
moulded ceiling and cornice, and the drawing room on the first floor,
lighted by large mullioned windows looking out on the Eastern
approach and Northern garden, having a quaint ceiling, supposed to be
the work of Italian artists, adorned with birds and animals in relief.
In one of the bedrooms on the first floor may be seen a handsomely
carved chimney-piece, on which are displayed the arms and crest
of the Gore family, flanked by two figures representing Justice
and Mercy; while in a small dressing room approached from the
gallery at the top of the house, the shield of Gore impaling
Tooker, is carved over the fireplace; and that of Gore impaling
Smith of Tedworth appears in the cornice of the plaster ceiling. From
the top of the Church tower a good bird's eye view may be obtained
of the North garden with its terraces and loggias, and also of the
adjoining outbuildings, which are admirably planned, and in keeping
with the mansion. It is possible that the carriage drive with its side
lawns originally formed the nuns garth or burying ground, for in the
course of excavation, several skeletons where here exhumed, one with

a piece of lead adhering to the breast bone. These with other remains were decently and reverently reinterred in the tombhouse at the N.W. corner of the Court aisle, where a memorial stone marking their last resting place, bears the following inscription, "In pious remembrance of the unknown dead, whose remains unwittingly disturbed lie beneath : may they rest henceforth in peace until The Great Day cometh."

On the lawn near the S.E. angle of the Church is a monument erected in 1850 by Montague Gore, Esq., to a favourite dog which, report says, he vainly endeavoured to bury in consecrated ground, and failing to obtain permission, excavated its grave under the adjoining wall. The inscription runs as follows, " To the memory of Pincher his lamented dog this monument was raised by his master, Montague Gore, as a last pledge of their long and reciprocal attachment, and as a mark of his deep regret for one who had been through many years his hearty companion by day, his watchful guard by night, in whom were displayed all the noblest qualities of his race, friendship without flattery, fidelity untainted by interest, gratitude abiding, unerring sagacity, love of his master undivided, intense, which age could not chill, nor lingering disease enfeeble, the passion that ruled his life, and was extinguished only by death. July, 1850." The

Facing the Court on the East, at the distance of about a quarter of a mile is a picturesque house known as Gratwicke Hall, formerly the Home farm, but converted in 1855 by John Henry Blagrave, Esq., into a residence, and named after his second son Gratwicke Blagrave, Esq., its present owner. Upon a stone let into the wall are the letters T. G. (Sir Thomas Gore) with the date 1674. The present tenant is Mrs. Bonville Were. At the back of the Hall, the Church path originally constructed as a carriage road, but so steep as to be almost impracticable, conducts to the village, in the centre of which stands a gabled farm house, which has evidently seen better days, judging from the old porch with its pediment and pillars of freestone, and inscription, W. G. (William Gore) 1687, while in a field behind, is the

BARROW HOUSE, BEFORE 1850.

Del. J. F. Wadmore, Esq., from pencil sketch by E. Bigg, Esq.

Cold Bath spring, rising at the base of a woody slope, and formerly flowing across the road into a tannery, until purchased by the Bristol Water Works Co.

About a hundred yards further on the left-hand, stands a quaint old-fashioned house approached by a flight of steps, with a miniature terrace garden, known as "Steps Farm." This was a private residence forty years ago belonging to the Hardwicke family, who lived there for several generations. The title deeds proving the conveyance of the property by Thomas Crossman and his wife in August, 1710 to Thomas Hardwicke and Catherine his wife, show that it was standing in the 44th year of Queen Elizabeth. The present owner Mrs. Bodham Castle inherited it from her father S. L. James, Esq., of East Harptree and Wrington, who married Miss Hardwicke in 1793.

At the South East extremity of the parish, divided by the Bridgwater road. are the three reservoirs of the Bristol Water Works Co., in the construction of which an old mansion known as Barrow House, with adjoining farm buildings was demolished in the year 1852. Here was the site of the old Manor house, for in a settlement dated June 15th, 1654, William Hasell and Johanne his wife are mentioned as owners of the "Old Court of Barrow Gurney," with 140 acres. Four sons are named, Cornelius, William, Richard, and Thomas, with Benjamin Tibbott and Richard Brooke *alias* Thomas, as Trustees. William Hasell, also spelt Hazle, died in 1680, and in the following year Cornelius Hazle sold the property to William Hendon. In 1778 it was purchased by William Prosser, gent, who a few years later conveyed it to Thomas Andrews,[63] in whose family it remained till the death of his daughter Mrs. E. M. Hogue[64] in 1831, when it was purchased by

[63] Mrs. Andrews died November 1813, and was buried in Barrow Church.
[64] See monument on N. wall of Nave, close to the Porch.

Anthony Blagrave, Esq., who sold it to the Bristol Water Works Co. From an unfinished pencil sketch by Edw. Bigg, Esq., of Clifton, it would seem that the house must have been of two stories, with square central tower, two wings, and verandahs running along the south or garden front. It was surrounded by tall trees, well kept pleasure grounds, and faced the high road. Its lodge, converted into a cottage, still remains.

The Bristol Water Works Co. was called into existence by Act of Parliament in 1846, when it was estimated that out of 130,000 inhabitants in Bristol and Clifton, only 5000 were supplied with pure water, the remainder being dependent on wells, in many cases unfit for use. The length of district now supplied is ten miles, its population 300,000, and the revenue derived from the sale of water £100,000 per annum. In or about 1847 the Cold Bath Spring in this parish was acquired, and its produce conveyed in pipes to Bristol, and in 1850 water from springs in the carboniferous lime stone was brought from the Mendips through ten miles of iron aqueduct to the reservoirs. The first and smallest of these was constructed in 1852, the second was finished in 1868, the third and largest in 1897.

The total capacity of the three reservoirs is about 850 million gallons, with a water acreage when all are full, of about 130. Water is also pumped into the reservoirs from deep wells in the sandstone formation at Chelvey. Adjoining the reservoirs are four filter beds, in area about three-quarters of an acre. The filtering medium consists of (1) a lower stratum of broken stone 2 feet thick, (2) six inches of finely broken stone, (3) a top layer of finely dressed sand from North Devon, two feet deep. The greatest care is taken to secure perfect filtration, and no expense has been spared to render the system complete.

At the Northern extremity of the parish is a pleasant country house, " Hillside," built a few years ago by P. H. George, Esq., and now the property of his widow.

The School premises occupy the site of an old mill, the large room having been erected by subscription during the incumbency of Rev. J. W. Hardman, L.L.D., 1862. The management is now in the hands of H. Martin Gibbs, Esq., who generously defrays all expenses, without cost to the parishioners. At present there are about 70 children on the books.

The Vicarage was until recently a[65] donative, or chaplaincy, terminable at the will of the patron,[66] with a stipend of £66 per annum, made up by a charge of £50 on the tithes, (which were commuted in 1839 at £245), and are the property of the Impropriator, J. G. Blagrave, Esq., and the interest on £510. 18s. 11d, bequeathed by Edward Gore, Esq. In 1881 the patronage was transferred to Antony Gibbs, of Tyntesfield, Esq., who by successive benefactions, met by grants from Queen Anne's Bounty, raised a capital sum of £4740, the gross income of which, together with the former amount represents £206 per annum. It is now in the patronage of H. Martin Gibbs, Esq., the present owner of Barrow Court.

The Parsonage or Vicarage house, which stands on high ground, encircled by fields, is flanked on the West by a row of fine sycamore trees, and approached by a lane originally a right of way to Gratwicke Hall, when a farm house. It is a picturesque building with gables, and ivy clad walls, and commands an extensive view of Bristol and Clifton, for the sake of which, regardless of an exposed Eastern aspect, it seems to have been designed. The present house was rebuilt, as an inscription over the West door records, in the year 1832, by a legacy from Edward Gore, Esq., while the cottage which preceded it, as an inscription records, was "the gift of Mrs. Mary Tooker, widdow, to my grandson William Gore, Esq., to be employed for the use of a Protestant minister for ever that shall supply the Cure at Barrow,

[65] A species of ecclesiastical property independent of episcopal control.
[66] Sir Thomas Gore, Kt., by his will 1675, gave £40 allowance to the minister to have the freedom to place, or displace him. Som. Wills, v, 86.

1679." It has experienced many vicissitudes, having served at different times, the purposes of a school, and a poor house.

The Chaplains serving the Chapelry prior to its becoming a Vicarage, being merely nominees of the Patron, and requiring no institution by the Bishop, are absent from Diocesan Records, and therefore their list is necessarily incomplete. Reference to the Registers, and other sources enables me to give the following imperfect return.

1510-11.	Ralph Bee, Curet.[67]
1515-16.	Robert Durant, at first Subdeacon.
1553.	Sir Richard Wryght, Priest.
1534.	Sir John Wanham, Curet.[68]
1666-71.	John Paull.
1671-74.	John Browne.
1676-79.	Thomas Potticary.
1679-89.	William Rawlins.
1689-94.	Samuel Still.
1694-96.	Matthew Morgan.
1696-1713.	Robert Sadler.
1714-33.	George Webber.
1733-83.	Charles Goddard.[69]
1783-89.	Thomas Goddard.[70]
1789-1812.	John Fallowfield.[71]
1812-29.	James Sparrow.[72]
1829-41.	William Charles Gore.[73]

[67] Som. Arch. Soc. Journ. xii, 86, 96, 109.
[68] Weaver's Wells Wills p. 10.
[69] Vicar of Portbury 1741, of Portbury-cum-Tickenham, 1764.
[70] Curate of Flax Bourton, buried here, æt 49, 1789.
[71] Curate of Flax Bourton, 1790, buried in vault of Barrow Church, 1812.
[72] Buried at Long Ashton, 1829.
[73] Died at S. Christophers, Jamaica, 1842, aged 40 years.

BARROW GURNEY CHURCH, 1821-1887 A.D.

1841-51.	George Martin Bullock.[74]
1851-58.	Thomas Foster Barrow.[75]
1858-61.	Philip B. Doyne.[76]
1861-65.	Joseph William Hardman.[77]
1865-69.	Gerard Moultrie.[78]
1869-81.	Edmund Lilley.[79]
1881-82.	John Richard Brougham.[80]
1882.	James Alfred William Wadmore.[81]

The Church, practically rebuilt through the munificence of the present patron, occupies the joint site of the old Church and Nuns' Chapel, and consists of Chancel with Vestry and Organ Chamber above it on the South, Nave with North Porch and Western Tower, and South or Court Aisle. Of the original Church standing at the beginning of the century, only a few mutilated fragments remain, as with the exception of the Tower, which was of 15th century date, and has been rebuilt, it was pulled down and re-erected in 1821, in the plain style of the Georgian era. It is said by Collinson to have comprised Chancel, Nave with North Porch, South Aisle, and Tower at the West-end. The[82] Chancel and North Porch however disappeared during the alterations, after which the Church consisted of two parallelograms of equal breadth, connected by an arcade of three Perpendicular arches, with tower and gallery at the West-end. The Court Aisle, the floor of which is nearly three feet below the adjoining external level on the South, was entered thence by a door and a flight of steps ; its pews placed longitudinally facing the pulpit, which was of picturesque design with old-fashioned

The Church.

[74] Fellow of S. John's Coll. Oxon, Vicar of Chalfont, S. Peter, 1863. Ob. 1892.
[75] S. Albans Hall, Oxford, M.A. Sec. S.P.G. 1840. Died and buried in London, 1869.
[76] T. C. D., M.A., 1841. Ob. 1861.
[77] T. C. D., L.L.D. Vicar and Founder of S. Katherine's, Felton, 1860-1885, buried there. Author of The " Parson's Perplexity," and other works.
[78] Ex. Coll., Oxon., M.A. 1856. Asst. Master, Shrewsbury, 1852. Vicar of Southleigh, Oxon., 1869, and Founder of S. James' College, 1873. Author of Hymns and Lyrics, &c. Ob. 1885, aged 55, buried at Southleigh.
[79] B.D., Worc. Coll., Oxon. Incumbent of Peckham Chapel. Ob. 1894, æt 86.
[80] T. C. D., M.A., 1865 Canon of Cloyne. Rector of Castlehaven, Co. Cork, 1886.
[81] Oriel Coll., Oxon., M.A.
[82] According to Collinson, the following shields were formerly in the Chancel windows.
   1 " *Barry wavy of six, argent and gules.*" Bayouse.
   2 " *Argent, two chevrons sable between three roses gules seeded or.*" Drew.
   3 " *Argent, three cinque foils per pale azure and gules.*" Choke.
   4 " *Argent, a chevron sable, between three lions dormant coward gules.*" Lyons.
   " *Quarterly per fesse indented argent and az., in the first quarter a mullet, gules.*" Acton. Coll. ii. p. 312.

sounding board, while the vestry, so called, consisted of a high square pew, in the South-east angle. The Belfry contained three bells two of which were cracked. The font, of Early English work, was rescued from the Churchyard, by the Rev. J. W. Hardman, and restored to its place.[83]

The present Church is built in the Decorated style, of Oolite stone quarried in the parish, with Bath-stone dressings, after the designs of F. Woodyer, Esq., and dedicated after the style and title of the Old Priory Church, to S. Mary the Virgin, and King Edward the Martyr.[84] Its exterior is best seen from the North. The Chancel and the Nave have buttresses between the windows, an ornamental band above relieving the blankness of the walls. The Consecration Cross is beneath the Eastern window. At the West-end, which is enriched with arcades, is a canopied niche, containing, with his name carved beneath, a figure of S. Benedict, to whose Order the Convent belonged. The Tower is square, with angle buttresses of four stages, and is finished above with a band of sunken quatrefoils and a beautiful perforated parapet. The Western window of two lights with hood moulding, and the Southern one are the only survivals of the older tower.

The Chancel, which rises two steps above the level of the Nave, is remarkable for its elaborately carved reredos towering from floor to roof, with crocketed pinnacles, delicate pediment, and carved niches, containing large figures of the Blessed Virgin Mary, and S. Edward, the former holding the Holy Child and lily emblem in her embrace, the latter a cup and dagger in his right, and a palm branch in his left hand, the emblems of his martyrdom. The floors of the Chancel and Sacrarium are of rich mosaic work, after a Roman pattern. The Altar is a fine slab of stone engraved with five crosses,

[83] It has since been presented to S. Katharine's, Pylle, Knowle, Bristol.

[84] The double dedication may be accounted for by the fact that it comprised within one building the Conventual, and the Parish Churches.

BARROW GURNEY CHURCH, RESTORED 1887-1891.

supported by an oak panelled frame, on pillars of ebony, with five crosses of ivory inlaid in its front. On a marble re-table are six brass vesper lights, and a magnificent embossed Cross set with large bloodstones. Immediately behind within a series of five arches, with marble columns, surmounted by a delicately carved entanglement of passion flowers, grapes, and ears of corn, is a sculptured group, representing the Institution by our Blessed Lord of the Holy Eucharist, and its administration to the faithful of all ages. In the central space stands the Saviour holding the Chalice, and delivering the Bread to S. Peter, while on the left are figures of the Blessed Virgin Mary, S. John, S. Etheldreda (first Queen Abbess), and Bishop Ken sometime Bishop of Bath and Wells; and on the right, S. Paul, S. Stephen, S. Alban first Saxon Martyr, and S. Augustine of Canterbury; while overhead are the cloud of witnesses, the Church Triumphant, Old Testament Saints, and adoring Angels. An arched piscina occupies the South-east angle, with sedilia for the Clergy; while on the opposite wall on a bracketed credence, stand the tall Eucharistic lights and the prayer desk when not in use, and hard by, the Bishop's throne and foot-stool of carved oak with crocketed back, having a mitre in its centre. Two stately Gospel candelabra by Singer of Frome, stand at the edge of the platform, bearing the respective inscriptions, "Evangelii Lux," "Salutis Dux."

The windows are filled with stained glass of the finest character, from the studio of C. E. Kempe, Esq., the gift, as an inscription on the South wall records, of Mrs. William Gibbs, of Tyntesfield, in her last hours. The subject of the East window is the "Tree of Life," our Blessed Lord occupying the central position, as "germen justum," surrounded by various Saints and worthies, representing different branches of the Catholic Church, in the following order :—

Left	Centre	Right
S. John the Evangelist.	Our Blessed Lord.	S. John the Baptist.
S. Edward the Confessor.	The Blessed Virgin Mary.	S. Mary Magdalene
S. Andrew.	S. Peter.	S. Benedict.
Moses.	S. Paul.	S. Ambrose.
S. Augustine of Hippo.	S. Gregory.	Sir Thomas More
S. Agnes.	S. Jerome.	Archbishop Laud.
David.		Sir Philip Sidney.
S. Margaret.		Bishop Andrewes.

The three other windows represent the Descent from the Cross ; the Burial in the Sepulchre; the Resurrection, Our Lord's appearance to the disciples at Emmaus, and to S. Thomas with the apostles, in the upper room.

Facing the Vestry door is a monumental mosaic of opaque glass framed in alabaster, erected in memory of the Rev. E. Lilley, a former incumbent, representing "The Charge to S. Peter," from the atelier of Messrs. Powell. The inscription runs :

"To the glory of God, and in memory of Edmund Lilley, B.D., Worcester College, Oxford, Vicar of this parish from 1869 to 1881 ; and of Louisa his wife, daughter of Michael Filton, R.N., who lie buried in this Churchyard ; this memorial is placed here by their relatives, parishioners and friends, Easter, 1895." And on the wall beneath in raised letters, is added " The Rev. E. Lilley bequeathed £200, the interest to be expended in goods every January, by the Vicar, amongst such poor of the parish as ordinarily attend the services of this Church, 1894." Affixed to one of the Chancel stalls, which are of oak with handsomely carved poppy heads, is a magnificent Processional Cross, with crystal bosses, the gift of H. M. Gibbs, Esq., Easter, 1896. A pointed doorway on the South conducts to the Vestry, and Organ Chamber above, which is corbelled out from the wall, and lighted by a small and elegant rose window. The Organ designed by Mr. Riseley, R.A.M., built by Messrs. Vowles of Bristol, is of two manuals and enclosed in an oak case.

The Vestry is fitted up with every convenience, wardrobes for Clergy and Choir, piscina for ablutions, library, and drawers for the Altar super-frontals, the handiwork of the Kilburn sisters, of which there is a complete sequence for the seasons. On the wall is a small piece of needlework in silver thread on crimson velvet, once part of an Altar cloth or pulpit hanging, with the initials M.G., and the date 1786, and between the windows, a stone bracket, supporting a small cross, originally presented to the Church by the Rev. Gerard Moultrie, but removed by his successor, and concealed beneath the Altar till it was brought to light during the restoration.

The handsome oaken screen which crosses the Chancel arch, is of unusual pattern, bearing on its top "the Rood," which rises from a semi-circular base, inscribed with the supplication, "By Thy Cross and Passion, Good Lord, deliver us." The Crucifix is flanked by figures of the Blessed Virgin Mary, and S. John, on raised pedestals. The wrought iron gates of the Chancel and South Aisle, are the work of Messrs. Filmore & Mason, Guildford.

Close to the screen on the North, a staircase in the wall, with groined roof, and circular shaft, gives access to the Pulpit, a richly carved work of Caen stone, with panels descriptive of the ministry of preaching. The subjects represented are The Sermon on the Mount (centre); Ezra, and S. John the Baptist (West); Noah, and S. Paul (East). On the opposite side, standing on a stone foot-pace, is the Lectern, of original design, handsomely carved in oak, constructed for a folio Bible of 1763. The Litany desk, of similar character, bears on the under side of the book ledge in carved letters, "To the Glory of God, the gift of the children of Barrow Gurney, September 12th, 1889." The windows on the North, which

are of "Decorated" work, are filled with stained glass by the artist
already named, and represent "The Agony in Gethsemane; The
Denial; The Mocking before Herod; and The Via Dolorosa.

On the wall is a series of monumental tablets in memory of
the Gore family, who lived here for many years, and whose remains
lie in the vaults beneath.

The Western Tower, which is set twelve feet further West than
the original structure, is entered from the Nave beneath a heavily
moulded arch of unusual height, its circular columns rising to that
of the groining within, which rests upon angle corbels. The bells
are rung from the floor, and have an iron guide to steady the ropes.
In the centre of the floor, lies a cracked mediæval bell, of the 15th
century, bearing in small Lombardic capitals the inscription
"Sancta Katerina ora pro nobis,"[85] It originally hung in the old
Tower with two others, bearing respectively the dates 1607 and 1628.

One of these has been re-cast, and forms No. 4 of the fine
ring of eight bells now located in the new Tower, the munificent
gift of H. M. Gibbs, Esq. Their aggregate weight is 3 tons 5 cwt.
Each bell bears a distinct motto, Treble, "Glory be to God on high";
Alto, "On Earth peace"; 3, "Goodwill to men "; 4, "We praise
Thee"; 5, "We bless Thee"; 6, "We worship Thee"; 7, "We
glorify Thee" ; Tenor, weighing 13½ cwt.—" We give thanks to Thee.
God save the Queen"; and in addition the following inscription :—
"Dedicated to the service of God by Henry Martin Gibbs, 1890.
J. A. W. Wadmore Vicar, R. Weeks, J. Vowles, Churchwardens."

The North Porch is of unusual design, projecting into the Nave.
Its oaken inner door, set within a trefoiled arch, is covered with
hammered iron work, two lions passant guardant stretching themselves across the foliage of a rose tree. Its inner roof is groined in
stone, and light is admitted by two small windows, set askew.

*³ Ellacombe's Church Bells of Somerset, p. 5 and Plate vii.

At the North-west corner of the Nave upon a marble pavement,
is the Font, of Caen stone, standing on three steps. It is of cup
shape, richly carved and surmounted by an elaborate oaken cover,
suspended from an iron bracket, and raised or lowered at will. In
the splay of the window on the North side, representing the Presentation of our Lord in the Temple, an inscription in Roman letters
denotes that the glass was inserted " in memory of Emily Metford
Wright, who fell asleep July 25th, 1891."

An arcade of three bays separates the Nave from the South Aisle,
the latter of which, judging from a quasi buttress at the North-
east corresponding with another on the South, and two blocked
doorways thought to be those of a rood staircase, but more
probably means of communication between the Church and the
adjoining Monastery, represents what was once the Chapel of the
Nuns. When, or by whom the arcade was erected we have no
knowledge, but if of post Reformation period, it is probably a
copy of an earlier structure. Its arches stand upon clustered
columns, the hood mouldings of which are terminated by sculptured
angels ; a dwarf stone screen with iron cresting, rising to the base
mouldings, serves to conceal the warming apparatus, while a wicket
gate of wrought iron at its Eastern end communicates with
the Nave ; the roof is of oak, coved and boarded, and the floor
of flag stones, many of which bear monumental inscriptions ;
the walls are enriched with a continuous series of lofty moulded
arches, supported by circular pillars with carved capitals ; in the
centre arch at the East, set back in a richly carved niche, is a representation of the Annunciation, and beneath it an alabaster
Reredos of seven arches, resting on pillars of red marble with
yellow caps and bases, and a backing of grey marble, surrounded
by a carved stone border, with the inscription—" Holy, Holy, Holy,
Lord God of Hosts." The Altar is of oak, set with a central cross :
it stands on an elevation of three marble steps, and is flanked with

hangings suspended from iron brackets; on the retable are an enamelled cross, and candlesticks, the latter bearing the words "God is my Light and my Salvation;" a stone seat for the Clergy and a credence niche, the head of which is ancient, are placed in the South-east angle; the South wall is pierced with three windows of two lights; the most Eastern, as an inscription in its splay records, was the gift of John Henry Blagrave, of Calcot Park, Reading, Esq., in memory of his wife Sarah, who died, 1865. In its tracery are the Arms of the Blagrave family, and below a representation of the Adoration of the Shepherds. The two other windows, containing in their heads the shields of Gibbs and Crawley-Boevey, represent the Adoration of the Magi, the Finding of our Lord in the Temple, the Flight into Egypt, and the workshop at Nazareth and were "the gift of Henry Martin Gibbs, of Barrow Court, in loving and reverent memory of his parents William and Matilda Blanche Gibbs, of Tyntesfield."

The blank spaces on the South and West walls have been utilised for monumental tablets, which have been carefully cleaned and coloured with the same reverent care which characterizes the entire restoration. Upon an elaborate oval slab, supported by marble pillars, and wreathed with pomegranates, above which are the arms and crest of Gore, is a Latin inscription in memory of William Gore, Esq., of Barrow Court, by his eldest son, Thomas Gore, Esq.[86] A moral sentence, "SapIens MorienDo LVChatVr," commonly known as a chronogram, supplies the date of his death, MDCLVVII, 1662. A pathetic inscription with the date 1658, and the shield of Bampfylde impaling Sydenham, commemorates Catherine Bampfylde, neé Sydenham,[87] a well-known Somersetshire family; she married Joseph Bampfylde, an officer in the Horse Guards during the reign of Charles II., and died in 1657. There is another tablet in memory of Ann Winter, relict of John Winter of Bath,[88] who died 1753, aged 58. On the West wall, are five monuments in memory

[86] Not mentioned by Collinson.

(1) William Gore, youngest son of William Gore Esq., who died in 1769, aged 68. (2) Elizabeth, wife of Edward Gore, Esq., ob. 1718. (3) John Sigismond Gore, ob. 1823, aged 21. (4) Rev. Charles and Harriett Gore, ob. 1841 and 1840, (5) Rev. William Charles Gore, ob. 1841.

Over the West door is a rich alabaster monument of Jacobean design, with marble columns and architrave, enclosing within a double recess, eleven kneeling figures, to the memory of Francis James, L.L.D., Chancellor of Wells, lord of the Manor, and owner of the Court house, who died, March, 1616, his wife and children. Upon the pediment are the arms of James, and above the figures the same impaling Gunter ; and also that of Gunter.

On a fragment near the altar is inscribed, " Here lyeth the body of Francis[89] (*son of Francis James who died the*) twentieth day of July, ano dni 1629."

Upon a flatstone forming the cover of their vault, near the East end of the aisle, are the names of several members of the Gore family, who lie buried beneath.

Upon another further South, " Hic jacet[90] Tho. Southworth armiger, legis consiliarius, et in societate graiorum doctor, pacis et quorum justitiarius, civitati Wellensi a memoria custos rotulorum

[87] Daughter of William and Mary Sydenham. William Sydenham, son of William and Mary, was Churchwarden, 1682. Arms. "*Or, on a bend gules three mullets argent,*" Bampfylde : impaling "*Argent, three rams passant, two and one, sable.*" Sydenham.

[88] John Winter was grandson of Henry Winter, of Clapton-in-Gordano, Esq., by Catherine, daughter of Sir Popham Southcote, Kt. The Winter shield which is wrongly placed on William Gore's monument, should read thus : – Quarterly. 1st and 4th "*Sable a fess and crescent in chief ermine,*" Winter. 2nd, "*Gules a chevron argent between three clarions or,*" Arthur. 3rd, "*Argent a chevron gules between three coots sable beaked and legged of the second,*" Southcote. on inescutcheon, "*Argent a lion passant gules between two bars sable, charged with three bezants, two and one, in chief three stags' heads cabossed of the third,*" Parker.

[89] The letters in Italics are conjecturally supplied from Register where there are two entries.—Francis James, July 20th, 1629 ; and (2) Francis James, October 15th, 1629. The latter may possibly be the nephew mentioned in Dr. James' Will.

[90] There is no entry of his burial in the Register. He was Recorder of Wells, 1608-9, and Member for the City in 1613 and 1619. His brother, Henry Southworth, was Lord of the Manor of Wyke Champflower, and was buried there 1625. The arms of the family are in one of the windows in the South Aisle of the Choir of Wells Cathedral. He was brother-in-law of Dr. Francis James, and is mentioned by him in his Will. Thomas married Jane, daughter of Nicholas Mynne of Norfolk. made a nuncupative Will dated 8th Sept., 1625, in which he is styled of Wells, and that he died at Barrow. A. J. Jewers, Wells Cathedral, pp. 44-45.

deputatus in Comitatu Som: qui obiit 8 die Septembris, anno domini 1625, ætatis suæ 61."

Upon another, so fractured as to be almost illegible:—

"She that in God did place her whole confidence,
In His Word, His Day, His Saints, His Sacraments,
And long'd for more than faith cd yield,
Is gone to heaven, with Him to be filled."

Here lyeth the remains of Mrs. Thomazin Thomas Williams[91] who, after a holy travel and long life of eighty-nine years and six months, died in March 7th, 1684."

There are a flagstone and two tablets in memory of William Briggs,[92] gent. ob. 1695, his son and daughter.

Inserted in the floor upon an incised stone slab, fractured, is a Cross Calvary ragulée, with an impaled shield in the corner, but having neither name or inscription.

Beyond the West-end of the Court aisle, upon the site of the Nave or Ante-Chapel of the Nuns' Church, a remarkable monument was discovered, believed to be an unique instance of a large tomb composed entirely of tiles, to protect which a small additional building was specially constructed. When first found, it was sufficiently perfect to reveal its entire design, but it has since by exposure to the air become injured beyond all possibility of restoration. In its centre a Latin cross formed of narrow black tiles lies within a bordure of small red squares set diamond-wise, carrying separately the Lombardic letters of the inscription ✠ DAME : IOANE ; DACTONE : GYST : ICY : DIEV : DE : SA : ALME : EYT : MERCY ✠ The background of the Cross is formed of heraldic shields, of which one half bore the coat of Acton[93]

[91] The Burial Register reads—"Mrs. Thomazin Thomas, who dyed the 7th inst., full of good works."

[92] William Briggs, was Churchwarden in the year 1690, and a cousin of Mrs. Mary Tooker. Somerset Wills v series, p. 88.

[93] "*Quarterly per fesse indented argent and azure, in first quarter a mullet gules.*" Acton of Chelvey.

[94] "Or, *three eagles displayed gules.*" Rodney of Rodney Stoke.

TOMB OF ENCAUSTIC TILES, BARROW GURNEY.

of Chelvey, the other that of Rodney [94] of Rodney Stoke and Back-well, conveying the impression that the deceased was a member of the latter family. Above, and below, are two large black bordered diamonds of sixteen tiles each, the lower one containing the arms of England four times repeated. On either side of the tomb is a broad band of ornamental tiles, amongst the varied patterns of which occurs, four times repeated, the following coat, "*three cinque foils (may be roses), with on a chief as many of the same*," which so far I have been unable to indentify, and two single tiles, bearing a '*maunch*,' the well-known cognizance of the de Mohuns of Dunster, the whole surrounded by a narrow border within black lines, containing the letters 𝔐. 𝔕. (Maria Regina) repeated alternately. This is interrupted on the North side by a second inscription of small detached Lombardic letters, [95] 𝔐𝔍𝔖𝔈𝔑𝔈𝔑𝔈. 𝔐𝔈𝔍. 𝔇𝔈𝔘𝔖. 𝔐𝔄𝔗𝔍𝔏𝔇𝔍, indicating a subsequent interment. The remaining space on either side is filled with ornamental pattern tiles, among which occur the arms of de Clare [96] and Berkeley [97] in quatrefoils, both separately and united, while around . the whole as an outer edging, a curved trifoliated ribbon, of which three tiles only remain in the South-west corner, completes the design.

The hatchments of the Rev. Charles Gore and his wife, who died 1840 and 1841, are preserved on the wall. Both bear the same shield, "Quarterly, 1 and 4, Gore, 2, Browne, 3, Smythe impaling Littell.

The Communion Plate, until superseded by the handsome set presented by the patron, Henry Martin Gibbs, Esq., at the Consecration of the Chancel, 1889, consisted of

---

[94] Matilda, daughter of Sir John Acton Kt., married first Sir Nicholas Poyntz, Kt., and secondly Roger Chandos; and dying 1631-32, may perhaps be the lady buried here.

[96] "*Three chevronels.*" Clare.

[97] "*A chevron between ten crosses pattee.*" Berkeley.

The Missing letters in these inscriptions were supplied by Bishop Kingdon. See also Som. Arch Journ., Vol xxix, p. 17, and Proceedings of Soc. of Antiquaries, May 1st, 1884.

1.—A deep Cup of plain silver, bearing the arms of Gore. " *Gules, a fesse between three crosses crosslet fitchée or*, crest, an *heraldic tiger rampant ducally gorged*" ; with hall mark, 1710.

2.—A small Paten with foot, bearing on its under surface, " Ex dono Gulielmi Gore Armigeri, in usum mensæ Dominicæ, 1713."

3.—Two-footed silver alms dishes, with gadrooned edges, and hall mark, 1712-13.

4.—A small modern alms-dish with cross engraved in the centre, the gift of F. Were, Esq., 1870.

5.—A modern glass water cruet:—

The handsome set already mentioned is of gilt, and comprises :

(*a*) A large and massive Chalice of mediæval shape, with repoussé work, representing bunches of grapes, the boss jewelled with sapphires, and the base ornamented with a Crucifix in coloured enamel.

(*b*) A Paten, enamelled underneath with wheat-ears, its base set with sapphires.

(*c*) A Flagon, with angels in repoussé, spout and lid. Around the rim, "Te laudamus Domine."

(*d*) A circular footed Ciborium, enamelled in colours, the lid crowned with open cross, set with a carbuncle.

(*e*) A Glass Cruet with gilt bands set with garnets, and enamelled foot and cover.

To these may be added a handsome gilt Alms dish with enamelled cross in centre, around the rim "Omnia sunt Tua, et de Tuis tibi dedimus," and a portable Altar, in the form of a box triptych, fitted with everything needful for the Communion of the sick; presented in memory of Miss E. M. Wright, A.D., 1893.

The Churchyard, which is entered by a picturesque Lych-gate of oak resting on stone piers, consists of two terraces laid out with flower beds, and divided by a dwarf wall. A separate entrance leads into the lower one, which was generously given by the Patron, and consecrated in 1884 for the burial of the parishioners, according to the rites and ceremonies of the Church of England. The upper portion, according to the Burial Register, contains the remains of more than 1175 bodies. A wheeled bier, with appropriate receptacle (which may be used in case of need as a mortuary cell), is also provided for the parishioners. The present Churchyard Cross replaces one[98] erected by Mrs. Alexander Hood, to the memory of her son, a pupil of the Rev. G. Moultrie, who died in the year 1867, and lies buried alongside. The upper stone of the Calvary, with a chamfered edge, formed the socket of a still earlier Cross,[99] two small fragments of which, subsequently discovered, have been cleverly reinserted in the head, the panels of which bear the following sculptures, *E.* The Crucifixion ; *W.* The Annunciation ; *N.* A crowned Abbess ; *S.* A Monk.

In the East and South boundary walls are a number of mutilated fragments from the old Church and Churchyard, one of which records the death of a centenarian :

> " Here lyeth two departed from this life,
> First the husband, next the wife ;
> A loved father and mother dear,
> Above a 100, that they were." [100]

Under the North wall of the Church is an old coffin lid of 14th century work, incised with a floriated Cross, which was found reversed in the year 1862, and stood for some time in the Tower porch.

---

[98] Re-erected S. E. corner of Churchyard. The base stone bore the following inscription—"To the honour of God, and in sweet memory of Francis F. Hood, this Cross is raised from the dust of three centuries, again to cast its shadow over the sleepers of Barrow Mynchin, Easter, 1868.

[99] This Cross has escaped the notice of Charles Pooley, Esq., F.S.A., in his collection of Old Stone Crosses of Somerset.

[100] This refers to John Horte, under whose name in the old Register, the following entry occurs, 1625, John Horte above 100.

There is little originality in the epitaphs, which were, as often as not, selected from the stone cutter's store book, but the following romantic inscription is worth recording. "To the memory of Joane Hunt and Samuel Hele."

> "Here lye we both bereaved of life
> Who thought to ha been husband and wife,
> 'Twas grim fac'd death that brought us hither,
> We lived in love, and lye together."

On a sarcophagus South of the Yew tree, is a Latin inscription to the family of Counsell, while a similar monument hard by, belongs to that of Norcott, (Northcote of Chewstoke.)

From the Registers, which are in an excellent state of preservation, it appears that the families of the Vowles (88) and Hazells, or Hasells, (65) are the two most largely represented. The earliest, a vellum-bound copy, contains entries of Baptisms and Burials 1590 to 1817; Marriages, 1593 to 1754. In separate folios are Baptisms, 1817 to 1893; Marriages, 1754 to 1814, (II.) 1817 to 1837; (iii) 1817 to present date. Burials 1817 to ditto. The earlier entries in the old folio are beautifully copied in one hand writing, from 1590—1671, by John Paull, minister from 1666—1671, and are evidently a transcript from some earlier Book. Amongst other miscellaneous entries, the following are deserving of notice:—

Marriage 1721, April 9th. Gyd Gad and Joice Collins, both of Dundry.

Burials 1630, May 29th. a poor Irishman, his name unknown.

1692, December 27th, Peregrina quædam sepulta est.

1698, April 20th, Puella projecta sepulta fuit.

while among singular names occur Bugfargus (servant of Sir Thomas Gore), Buggossi, spelt also Buggass and Buggis, Ægidius, Blandina, Melenda, Brisilla, Katabella, Jephtha-ey-fald.

From the Churchwarden's accounts, which extend from 1784 to
1821, it appears that the Sacrament of the Lord's Supper was
administered four times a year, the charge for bread and wine
varying from 3/- to 7/6. In 1836, the celebration was monthly,
and continued so till 1882. There is now a weekly celebration,
as also on Holy days, and thrice at the Great Festivals. An
entry varying from 5/- to 11/- appears annually between 1783
and 1838, for a "Book of Articles;" these were Articles of
enquiry prior to the Visitation of the Bishop or Archdeacon,
now transmitted by post, but formerly delivered by hand, the
apparitor's fee varying in amount according to the rank of the
visitor. The two following entries are worthy of preservation:
1821, October 17th, "This old Church taken down to be re-built,
being two years and one month in building,[101] November, 23rd,
1823, finished and opened for service this day, by Mr. Sparrow."
and "1824, paid John Williams for thatching the gallery 8/6;
helm for ditto, 12/-."

There are two Charities. That known as "Ascension Money,"
arises from a bequest of Edward Gore, of Barrow Court, Esq., in
1801, of £200, the interest to be expended in payment of 20/-
to the Curate of the Church of Barrow for preaching a sermon
at the same Church on Ascension Day, of 3/- to the Clerk, the
residue to be distributed amongst the poor of Barrow, usually called
"the second poor," i.e—those not in receipt of parish pay.[102]

The Rev. Edmund Lilley by his will 1892, proved 1894,
bequeathed to the Vicar for the time being, £200, to be invested
at his discretion; the income to be distributed annually in
January, in coals, flannel, blankets or clothing, amongst such of

[101] The expenses were evidently defrayed by one of Gore family, probably the Rev. Charles
Gore, as the statement of Accounts is left blank.

[102] Query. Is it a corruption of "Sick and Poor?" The present Trustees are Earl Temple,
H. M. Gibbs, Esq., and Rev. Prob. Burbidge.

the poor of the Parish, who ordinarily attend the services in the Parish Church.[103]

An earlier benefaction, of which no particulars are known, supposed to have been a charge upon the Estate of William Gore, Esq., of Barrow Court, amounting to £4 per annum, was acknowledged and paid by the Rev. George Gore, till 1857, when it lapsed.

[103] The above sum was handed over to the Charity Commissioners, and invested in Consols. The income therefrom is £5. 6s. 4d.